GEMSTONES

GEMSTONES

CHARTWELL
BOOKS, INC.

Published by Chartwell Books
A Division of Book Sales Inc.
114 Northfield Avenue
Edison, New Jersey 08837
USA

ISBN 0-7858-0972-4

This book is produced by
Quantum Books Ltd
6 Blundell Street
London N7 9BH

Project Manager: Rebecca Kingsley
Project Editor: Judith Millidge
Design/Editorial: David Manson
Andy McColm, Maggie Manson

The material in this publication previously appeared in
Rocks, Shells, Fossils, Minerals and Gems,
Crytsal Identifier, The Gem and Mineral Collection

QUMSPGM
Set in Futura
Reproduced in Singapore by Eray Scan
Printed in Singapore by Star Standard Industries (Pte) Ltd

Contents

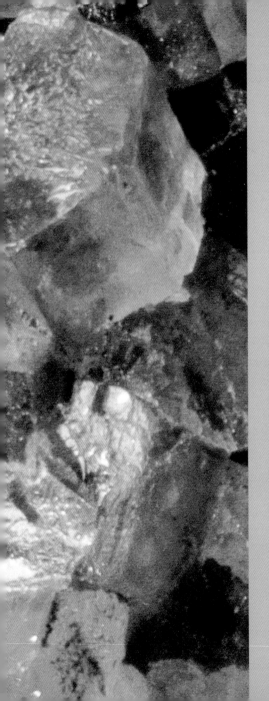

GORGEOUS GEMSTONES

Regular, beautiful and exact —
gemstones have excited desire
and imagination for thousands of
years. Created by chance in an
unbelievably hostile environment,
their crystals have a form precise
enough to delight scientists, colors
bold and variable enough to
inspire artists, and a chemical
make-up as unpredictable and
intriguing as the weather.

Supernatural Gemstones

It is little wonder that the beauty of gems, their regularity and hidden powers have guided and haunted people since the dawn of time. Gems could be carried, would not run away or rot — and could be easily hidden.

HIDDEN POWERS

Without even a basic understanding of nature, early civilizations unsurprisingly thought that gem crystals held supernatural powers. Crystals are also believed to have been amongst the first materials that primitive peoples chipped into crude but effective weapons.

Simultaneously, they have been used for centuries to ward off evil spirits and provide strength to the weak. Crowns of kings and queens, tokens of love, affection and good luck are frequently embellished with gemstones. They are also a convenient way of storing and displaying wealth.

Left. Labradorite is associated with eruptive and metamorphic rocks.

Above. Opal is hardened jelly found filling the cavities in rocks.

HEALING GEMSTONES

Today, many people still hold the belief that gem crystals in their elegance and stability, contain the strength to guide or correct any wandering or wayward spirits. There is little doubt that they have often provided hope and relief to the mentally or physically distressed. Equally it is clear that the recent renewed interest in the medical benefits of crystals is caused by disenchantment with established medical practices.

DEFINED BY SCIENCE

Now we have a more complete and scientific understanding of gem crystals. They can most simply be defined as naturally occurring inorganic minerals which take on a uniform shape within a specific structure. Their physical and chemical properties are defined by the elements which make up each individual crystal. But our greater knowledge of science has not detracted from the interest in their hidden powers.

Gemstone Formation

How is it that something as perfect and beautiful as a gemstone can come from the Earth where it is found amongst unimpressive looking rock formations?.

CRYSTAL FORMATION

With few exceptions, minerals are not created, but grow from a tiny nuclei in a solution into crystals. It is unclear what causes the initial nuclei. It may be atoms, normally being agitated at high frequency, exist by chance for an instant in the exact orientation that they would assume if they were solid. This chance occurrence may start the whole crystal growth process.

The growth of crystals at this stage is similar to that of a pearl which develops layer by layer from a grain of sand within an oyster. It is hard to believe that crystals form one atom at a time, but this process takes place in three dimensions and is repeated thousands of times a second. Depending on the crystal size, they can take anything from a day to a year to be completed.

Left. Agates are made in a volcanic environment from gas-created voids.

Above. Smoky quartz crystals are found in hydrothermal veins in Brazil.

UNDER PRESSURE

Gemstone crystals are formed from gases, aqueous solutions or molten rock which are usually created far below the Earth's surface. Sometimes they are reformed from previously solid material which has been heated and pressurized until it liquifies, only resuming a solid state when the pressure or heat is removed. Such reformed crystals may not look like their original form due to a change in the heat or pressure in their growth environment.

HYDROTHERMAL ACTION

Crystals are often formed as a result of hydrothermal action. A super-hot solution heavily charged with chemical elements is forced by high temperature through micro-cracks and veins. As this solution is displaced, its pressure and temperature are dissipated. When the conditions are less 'turbulent', gem crystals will grow out of the solution. Most crystals owe their existence to these super-hot activities originating deep within the Earth's crust.

The Growth of a Gemstone

The size of a gemstone crystal depends on the rate of growth: the slower they grow, the larger they will be. This may be due to evaporation, a cooling off of the solution or the bleeding off of pressure.

SLOW GROWTH

Sometimes the results of a slow crystal growth are spectacular. In Brazil, a beryl crystal weighing 200 tons was found and in Siberia, a milky quartz crystal of 13 tons was uncovered. Slow growth rate also helps the crystal to be shaped more regularly because the atoms have more time in which to assume some orderly arrangement.

FACE GROWTH

The faces of gem crystals do not necessarily grow at the same speed. This difference in the rate of growth, if very pronounced will result in elongated crystals. A faster accumulation of atoms in one direction, due possibly to a strong electrical attraction will be exaggerated as the atoms are being attracted to a small face-end rather than to a long side.

Left. Milky quartz is the rougher more compact formation of amethyst.

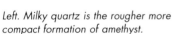

Above. High quality mined crystals of tourmaline are cut into gemstones.

SOLID BASE GROWTH

Similarly if a crystal grows from a solid base, as is so often the case with amethyst and halite, only half of the crystal is properly in a good position to be able to receive new unit-cells. However, it is really astonishing that these crystals are not more frequently completely malformed and irregular in shape.

REGULAR SHAPES

Even under ideal conditions, few minerals do not form regular shapes, but simply assume a more rigid form of the liquid phase. When such minerals are formed from a gel, they are usually made of tiny crystals which, given time and stable conditions, will join together to form solid masses or aggregates.

13

Distinguishing Gemstones

One of the truly fascinating aspects of gemstone crystals is that despite their seemingly limitless shapes they belong to one of only seven classifications. These are referred to in the text with the following icons.

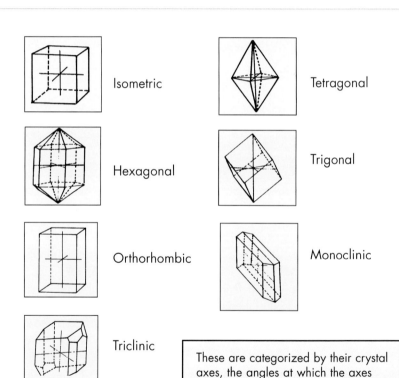

Isometric

Tetragonal

Hexagonal

Trigonal

Orthorhombic

Monoclinic

Triclinic

These are categorized by their crystal axes, the angles at which the axes radiate from the crystal's central point of intersection and the planes in which these axes lie.

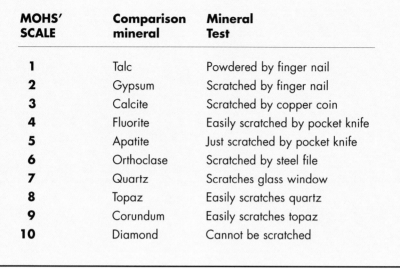

MOHS' SCALE	Comparison mineral	Mineral Test
1	Talc	Powdered by finger nail
2	Gypsum	Scratched by finger nail
3	Calcite	Scratched by copper coin
4	Fluorite	Easily scratched by pocket knife
5	Apatite	Just scratched by pocket knife
6	Orthoclase	Scratched by steel file
7	Quartz	Scratches glass window
8	Topaz	Easily scratches quartz
9	Corundum	Easily scratches topaz
10	Diamond	Cannot be scratched

HARDNESS

Hardness, an inherent and easily determined mineral characteristic, is measured using a resistance to scratching method known as 'Mohs' Scale', after Freidrich Mohs (1773–1839) a Viennese mineralogist. Mohs arranged ten minerals in order of hardness with 1 being the softest and 10 being the hardest. Each mineral can be scratched by the one below it in the scale: 1and 2 are 'soft'; 3 to 6 are 'medium-hard'; 6 to 8 are termed 'hard'; and 8 to 10 have 'precious-stone' hardness. The scale is shown in the table above.

SPECIFIC GRAVITY

The specific gravity of a gem crystal is a measure of its density (it is sometimes referred to as its relative density). It is defined as weight per unit volume, i.e. the ratio of the weight of an object to the weight of an equal volume of distilled water. Consequently a gem with a specific gravity of 4 is four times as heavy as the same volume of water. The density of a material is often used reliably to separate worthless minerals from the valuable, especially if there is a large respective difference in their specific gravities.

GEMSTONE CRYSTALS

Over 5,000 years ago in Ancient Egypt, the Pharaohs employed thousands of slaves to operate the first commercial gemstone mines. To this day, gemstones are sought after for their endurance and beauty and, although more commonplace materials such as rock salt now come from crystal sources, high quality crystals continue to be used as gemstones throughout the world.

DIAMOND

The value of a diamond as a gemstone is based on the 'four Cs': color, clarity, cut and carat (weight). Only 20% of all diamonds are suitable for gemstones, the rest being used in industry as an abrasive for drilling, boring or grinding. The diamond's most distinctive features are its hardness and sparkle, which are unmatched by any other crystal.

Mohs' Hardness 10.
Specific gravity 3.47–3.55.
Crystal structure Isometric.
Color Colorless, yellow tones, blue, brown-green, red, violet.
Range South Africa.

MOHS'	SPEC GRAV	
10	3.55	

RUBY

Lower quality crystals are powdered and used as high-quality cutting and polishing mediums. They tend to occur in dolomitic type limestones which have become marble-like rocks. Most rubies are mined from alluvial deposits. The color is often uneven within the crystal and they have a soft, silky sheen due to the inclusion of minute rutile crystals.

Mohs' Hardness 9.
Specific gravity 3.97–4.05.
Crystal structure Hexagonal.
Color Shades of red.
Range Burma, Thailand, Afghanistan, Australia, Brazil, Cambodia, India, USA.

MOHS'	SPEC GRAV	
9	4.05	

SAPPHIRE

Sapphires derive their color from iron within the stone and are formed as crystals in marble, basalt and pegmatite. The origin determines the color of the stone: Australian stones are a deep blue; Sri Lankan stones are a patchy blue color; while Kashmir stones are a milky cornflour blue.

Mohs' Hardness 9.
Specific gravity 3.99–4.00
Crystal structure Hexagonal.
Color Black, purple, violet, shades of blue, green, yellow, orange.
Range Kashmir in India, Australia, Brazil, Burma, Cambodia, Kenya.

MOHS'	SPEC GRAV
9	4.00

CHRYSOBERYL

Green chrysoberyl, alexandrite, and honey-yellow cat's-eye are highly prized gemstones. Alexandrite is distinctive and is green in natural light and red in artificial light. Chrysoberyls tend to be sensitive to chemical attack by alkalis and can change color when heated.

Mohs' Hardness 8.5.
Specific gravity 3.7–3.72.
Crystal structure Orthorhombic.
Color Green, yellow, gray, brown, colorless.
Range Brazil, Burma, Madagascar, Norway, Sri Lanka, Tanzania, Russia, USA.

MOHS'	SPEC GRAV
8.5	3.72

TOPAZ

Topaz is a highly prized gemstone, but
has lost some of its popularity to citrine
quartz. Topaz from Brazil is often heat-
treated to give pink topaz. The crystals
are mostly found in alluvial deposits and
the most common crystals have a yellow
color with a red tint. Deep yellow are the
most valuable.

Mohs' Hardness 8.
Specific gravity 3.52–3.56.
Crystal structure Orthorhombic.
Color True topaz, pink topaz, blue topaz
and colorless topaz.
Range Brazil, Afghanistan, Nigeria,
Japan, Mexico, Namibia, Burma, Russia.

MOHS'	SPEC GRAV	
8	3.56	

TAAFEITE

This is an extremely rare mineral which
is of interest as it is the first mineral to
have been identified when already cut
as a gemstone. The first specimen was
found in 1945, by Count Taafe of Dublin,
amongst a jeweler's box of mixed stones.
Resembling a spinel it weighed 1.419
carats but was doubly refractive,
whereas spinel, is singly refractive.

Mohs' Hardness 8.
Specific gravity 3.62.
Crystal structure Hexagonal.
Color Pale mauve, ruby-red,
sapphire-blue.
Range Sri Lanka, China, Russia.

MOHS'	SPEC GRAV	
8	3.62	

SPINEL

Spinel has been used in jewelry for centuries, set alongside diamonds and rubies. The spinel crystals form in limestones, where there are deposits of manganese or aluminium. If iron is present they will have red hues. Blue hues indicate the presence of chrome. Crystals can be transparent or opaque with a vitreous luster.

Mohs' Hardness 8.
Specific gravity 3.58–3.61.
Crystal structure Isometric.
Color Pink, red, violet-red, pale lilac, blue, violet-blue and black.
Range Afghanistan, Burma.

MOHS'	SPEC GRAV	
8	3.61	

AQUAMARINE

The name comes from Latin and means 'water from the sea'. A traditional good luck charm of sailors, the rich blue crystals are the most highly prized as gems. The crystals are usually found in alluvial deposits, where their hardness and resistance to chemical attack have allowed them to remain almost unaltered.

Mohs' Hardness 7.5–8.
Specific gravity 2.67–2.71.
Crystal structure Hexagonal.
Color Pale blue to light blue-green to light green.
Range Afghanistan, Brazil, USA, Russia, Madagascar.

MOHS'	SPEC GRAV	
8	2.71	

BERYL

Beryls are characteristic of granite and pegmatitic rocks where they often occur as large crystals. Due to their hardness and resistance to chemical attack, beryls often occur as unaltered crystals in alluvial deposits. It is considered to be a semi-precious gemstone, having a vitreous luster.

Mohs' Hardness 7.5–8.
Specific gravity 2.65–2.75.
Crystal structure Hexagonal.
Color Pale green.
Range Brazil, Czech Republic, India, Madagascar, Russia, USA.

MOHS'	SPEC GRAV	
8	2.75	

BIXBITE

Due to its rarity and distinctive color, bixbite is a relatively highly valued semi-precious gemstone. It has not been commercially imitated or produced synthetically. Unlike other crystals of the beryl group, bixbites are found in effusive magmatic rhyolite rocks.

Mohs' Hardness 7.5–8.
Specific gravity 2.65–2.75.
Crystal structure Hexagonal.
Color Ruby-red, strawberry, violet hues.
Range Only in the USA.

MOHS'	SPEC GRAV
8	2.75

GOLDEN BERYL

One of the less valuable gems from the beryl group, it is of marginal value and is not produced synthetically or imitated. As with most other crystals from the beryl group, golden beryl is associated with igneous activity. The yellow pigment is thought to be due to iron contained within the crystal structure.

Mohs' Hardness 7.5–8.
Specific gravity 2.65–2.75.
Crystal structure Hexagonal.
Color Canary yellow to golden yellow.
Range Brazil, USA, Sri Lanka, Madagascar.

MOHS'	SPEC GRAV
8	2.75

EMERALD

The emerald has long been valued as a gemstone, with deep-green crystals commanding the highest prices. Emeralds contain inclusions, a sign of authenticity, and do not necessarily detract from their value. Synthetic emeralds are now being produced with inclusions similar to those in natural crystals.

Mohs' Hardness 7.5–8.
Specific gravity 2.67–2.78.
Crystal structure Hexagonal.
Color Bright green, light green, yellow-green or dark green.
Range Colombia, Africa, Brazil, India, Australia, Tanzania, Pakistan, Russia.

MOHS'
8

SPEC GRAV
2.78

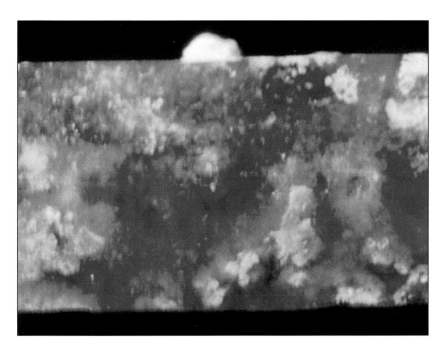

MORGANITE

Named after the American banker John Morgan, it is a strongly colored crystal which is much valued as a gemstone. Morganite crystals occur in or near pegmatite veins. Low color specimens can be heat-treated to improve them to aquamarines. The crystals, which occur as long prisms, have a glassy luster.

Mohs' Hardness 7.5–8.
Specific gravity 2.67–2.78.
Crystal structure Hexagonal.
Color Bright green, light green, yellow-green or dark green.
Range Colombia, Africa, Brazil, India, Australia, Tanzania, Pakistan, Russia.

MOHS'
8

SPEC GRAV
2.78

SILLIMANITE

Sillimanite is often fibrous and has the same chemical composition as kyanite and andalusite and is therefore polymorphic. Crystals occur in parallel groups as long slender prisms which do not have distinct terminations. The colors seen down the three principal optical directions are pale green, dark green and blue.

Mohs' Hardness 7.5.
Specific gravity 3.25.
Crystal structure Orthorhombic.
Color Violet-blue, grayish-green.
Range Burma, Sri Lanka, USA.

MOHS'	SPEC GRAV	
7.5	3.25	

DANBURITE

Danbrite is of marginal value as a gemstone, despite its hardness. The crystals are usually found in fissures and in lining lithoclase. The crystals tend to be either colorless or pink and have a greasy luster. The boron in the crystal's make-up will color a flame green, and it can easily be fused into a colorless glass.

Mohs' Hardness 7.5.
Specific gravity 3.25.
Crystal structure Orthorhombic.
Color Colorless, pink, or pale yellow.
Range Burma, Sri Lanka, USA.

MOHS'	SPEC GRAV	
7.5	3.25	

ANDALUSITE

Quality crystals are sometimes cut into gems, especially when they display a greenish or reddish color. It is a characteristic mineral of low-pressure metamorphic rocks. Rich in aluminium and poor in calcium, potassium and sodium. They have a modest luster.

Mohs' Hardness 7–7.5.
Specific gravity 3.12–3.2.
Crystal structure Orthorhombic.
Color Light-yellowish brown, bottle-green, light brownish-pink, grayish-green.
Range Spain, Australia, Brazil. Burma, Canada, Sri Lanka. USA.

MOHS'	SPEC GRAV
7.5	3.20

INDICOLITE

Indicolite crystals commonly occur in greisen and pegmatites, where they grow due to magmatic intrusions. Crystals also occur in sedimentary rocks as branch-like or authigenic grains. Named after the color indigo, indicolite is the blue variety of tourmaline, but crystals can also be greenish-blue.

Mohs' Hardness 7–7.5.
Specific gravity 3.02–3.26.
Crystal structure Hexagonal.
Color Blue or greenish-blue.
Range Brazil, Madagascar, Namibia, Russia, USA.

MOHS'	SPEC GRAV	
7.5	**3.26**	

IOLITE

Iolite is formed in areas of contact metamorphism and less frequently in silica- and alumina-rich granite or rhyolitic rocks. The names is derived from its sometimes violet color. It is sometimes confused with quartz. Unlike quartz, it is fusible in thin sections and is insoluble in acid.

Mohs' Hardness 7–7.5.
Specific gravity 2.53–2.66.
Crystal structure Orthorhombic.
Color Dark blue to light blue, with gray a common additional hue.
Range Brazil, Burma, Canada, Finland, India, Sri Lanka, Namibia, USA.

MOHS'	SPEC GRAV	
7.5	**2.66**	

PYROPE

The name pyrope gets its name from the Greek word *pyropos,* meaning fiery. It is a moderately valuable semi-precious gemstone, with the darkest crystals being the most common. Pyrope is typically formed in peridotite, as well as in kimberlite. Due to their resistance to weathering, pyropes are often found in alluvial or secondary deposits.

Mohs' Hardness 7–7.5
Specific gravity 3.65–3.87.
Crystal structure Isometric.
Color Deep red.
Range Argentina, Brazil, South Africa, Mexico, Czech Republic, Tanzania, USA.

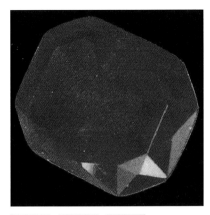

MOHS'	SPEC GRAV
7.5	3.87

STAUROLITE

Staurolite frequently occurs in cruciform-twinned crystals and is worn as religious jewelry. The crystals often have a rough earthy coating which hides their reddish-brown to black interior. They are usually found embedded in kyanite or schist as flat elongated crystals.
Semi-opaque with a resinous luster.

Mohs' Hardness 7–7.5
Specific gravity 3.7–3.8.
Crystal structure Monoclinic.
Color Deep wine-red to brown or yellow.
Range Germany, Scotland, Switzerland, USA, France.

MOHS'	SPEC GRAV
7.5	3.80

RUBELLITE

Modestly priced and with no
inclusions, rubellite crystals usually
form in association with igneous and
metamorphic activity. Crystals occur in
greisen and pegmatites. The color is
a distinctive feature but can sometimes
be a little subdued.

Mohs' Hardness 7–7.5.
Specific gravity 3.02–3.26.
Crystal structure Hexagonal.
Color Violet-red, pink.
Range Burma, Sri Lanka,
Madagascar, USA, Brazil, Russia.

MOHS'
7.5

SPEC GRAV
3.26

TOURMALINE

Tourmaline is named after the Sinhalese word for hard rocks. High quality, crystals are cut into gemstones. Color zoning is common, varying from green, at the base, to red at the apex. Zoned stones are often sliced and polished as ornamental objects.

Mohs' Hardness 7–7.5.
Specific gravity 3.02–3.26.
Crystal structure Hexagonal.
Color Pink, fiery red and deep green. Pale colors can be heat treated to intensify the color.
Range Burma, Brazil, Sri Lanka, USA, Mozambique, Madagascar.

MOHS'	SPEC GRAV	
7.5	**3.26**	

VERDELITE

The name comes from the Italian word for 'green stone'. The crystals range in color through the green spectrum and only the mid-range of colors are considered suitable for cutting into gems. They are associated with igneous rocks, but are also found in alluvial deposits.

Mohs' Hardness 7–7.5.
Specific gravity 3.02–3.26.
Crystal structure Hexagonal.
Color Light-green to emerald-green to deep-green.
Range Brazil, Mozambique, USA, Russia, Sri Lanka, Tanzania, Namibia.

MOHS'	SPEC GRAV	
7.5	**3.26**	

CITRINE

Most commercial citrines are heat-treated amethysts or smoky quartz. Citrine is widely used as an imitation of topaz. Larger citrine crystals are prismatic with pyramid ends. The crystals will turn white if heated and dark brown if exposed to X-rays. Cut crystals display good luster.

Mohs' Hardness 7.
Specific gravity 2.65.
Crystal structure Hexagonal.
Color Pure yellow to dull yellow, honey or brownish yellow.
Range Brazil, France, Madagascar, USA, Russia.

MOHS'	SPEC GRAV	
7	**2.65**	

AMETHYST

This is the most highly prized form of quartz. High quality crystals are still used as a semi-precious gem. Amethyst crystals always grow from a base. The color is due to the presence of ferric iron. The distribution of color bands and wavy parallel lines distinguishes amethysts from crystals of a similar appearance.

Mohs' Hardness 7.
Specific gravity 2.63–2.65.
Crystal structure Hexagonal.
Color Violet, purple or pink.
Range Brazil, Australia, Canada, USA, Russia, India, South Africa, Sri Lanka.

MOHS'	SPEC GRAV	
7	**2.65**	

MILKY QUARTZ

Often cut into beads, ornaments and *objets d'art,* milky quartz is found in pegmatites and hydrothermal veins. The distinctive color is due to the inclusion of numerous bubbles of gas and liquid in the crystal. Milky quartz is the rougher, more compact formation of amethyst. Common in the earth's surface, one find weighed 14.5 tons.

Mohs' Hardness 7.
Specific gravity 2.65.
Crystal structure Hexagonal.
Color Milky.
Range Russia, Europe, Brazil, USA, Namibia, Madagascar.

MOHS'	SPEC GRAV	
7	**2.65**	

ROCK CRYSTAL

Quite common, rock crystal is often carved into *objets d'art* or made into jewelry. In the past it has been used for optical and piezo-electrical purposes, now synthetic crystals are used. Rock crystal is crystallized directly from magma, in pegmatites, and low temperature hydrothermal regions. It is birefringent and distinguishable from glass by its absence of air bubbles.

Mohs' Hardness 7.
Specific gravity 2.65.
Crystal structure Trigonal.
Color Colorless, transparent.
Range Brazil and throughout the world.

MOHS'
7

SPEC GRAV
2.65

ROSE QUARTZ

Much valued as an ornamental material because of its attractive color and rarity. It is not popular as it has a tendency to be brittle, and well-formed crystals are rare. The color is caused by traces of manganese or titanium and is milky rather than perfectly transparent. The crystal is often cracked and only recently have any been found with flat sides.

Mohs' Hardness 7.
Specific gravity 2.65.
Crystal structure Hexagonal.
Color Strong to pale pink.
Range Brazil, Madagascar, USA.

MOHS'	SPEC GRAV	
7	2.65	

SMOKY QUARTZ

Often cut into gemstones or *objets d'art*, crystals weighing up to 670lb have been found in hydrothermal veins in Brazil. Its distinctive smoky characteristic is possibly due to rock crystal being subjected to natural radiation. Named for its smoky color, it can turn yellow when heated, then turn white. Quality crystals often contain rutile inclusions.

Mohs' Hardness 7.
Specific gravity 2.65.
Crystal structure Hexagonal.
Color Strong to pale pink.
Range Brazil, Madagascar, USA.

MOHS'
7

SPEC GRAV
2.65

TIGER-EYE

Often used for carving-boxes and other ornamental items. The crystals are formed from fine fibrous quartz aggregates which have had the criodolite altered to a yellow color. The golden hue is due to the presence of brown iron. The fibers making up the stripes are concentrated into semi-parallel groupings.

Mohs' Hardness 7.
Specific gravity 2.64–2.71.
Crystal structure Hexagonal.
Color Gold-yellow to gold-brown stripes on an almost black background.
Range South Africa, Australia, Burma, India, USA.

MOHS'	SPEC GRAV	
7	2.71	

QUARTZ CAT'S EYE

This material is not very valuable, despite its attractiveness. It is usually cut into round polished pieces for necklaces or pendants. Quartz cat's eye is formed from fluids associated with intrusive magmatic phenomena. Often confused with chrysoberyl cat's eye, the material is sensitive to acids.

Mohs' Hardness 7.
Specific gravity 2.65.
Crystal structure Hexagonal.
Color Semi-transparent but becomes greenish-gray or green when ground.
Range Burma, India, Sri Lanka, Germany.

MOHS'	SPEC GRAV	
7	2.65	

SPODUMENE

There are two varieties: kunzite and hiddenite. Spodumene occurs as flattened prisms characterised by vertical striations and irrregular terminations. The crystals exhibit strong cleavage in two directions. Cutting is difficult because of the strong cleavage and the shape of the crystals.

Mohs' Hardness 7.
Specific gravity 3.18.
Crystal structure Monoclinic.
Color Kunzite is lilac-pink; hiddenite is bright green.
Range Brazil, USA, Madagascar, Burma.

MOHS'	SPEC GRAV	
7	3.18	

BROWN QUARTZ

Brown quartz is found as hexagonal prisms. It is doubly refractive but has no characteristic absorption spectrum or luminescence under ultraviolet light or X-rays. It often has rutile inclusions, which add to the beauty and interest of the stone. It is often faceted for gemstones or carved for *objets d'art*.

Mohs' Hardness 7.
Specific gravity 2.65.
Crystal structure Trigonal.
Color Yellow-brown, gray-smoke to almost black.
Range Swiss Alps, USA, Japan, Spain, Australia.

MOHS'	SPEC GRAV	
7	2.65	

GROSSULAR

Green and yellow tinted grossular crystals are often cut and sold as gemstones. They are associated with metamorphism and are usually weathered from their host rock and found in gem gravels. The coloration is due to iron pigments and chrome within the crystal structure. They vary from semi-opaque to transparent.

Mohs' Hardness 6.5–7.5.
Specific gravity 3.58–3.69.
Crystal structure Isometric.
Color Green, yellow, copper-brown, cinnamon-brown, orange.
Range Canada, Kenya, South Africa, Sri Lanka, Tanzania, Mexico, USA.

MOHS'
7.5

SPEC GRAV
3.69

SPESSARTITE

Gem quality crystals are rare, but when they do occur, they are usually well-formed. They are generally formed by low-grade metamorphic rocks. The crystals are unusual in that they display a high degree of hardness and density. They are semi-opaque or transparent.

Mohs' Hardness 6.5–7.5.
Specific gravity 4.12–4.20.
Crystal structure Isometric.
Color Orange-pink, orange-red, red-brown, brownish-yellow.
Range Burma, Sri Lanka, Brazil, USA, Mexico, Sweden, Madagascar.

MOHS'	SPEC GRAV
7.5	4.20

ALMANDINE

Crystals free of inclusions and internal cracks are sometimes cut into gemstones. The crystals are common in medium-grade metamorphic or contact metamorphic areas. Cut crystals have a brilliant luster, but their transparency is often marred by excessive depth of color.

Mohs' Hardness 6.5–7.5.
Specific gravity 3.95–4.2.
Crystal structure Isometric.
Color Red with a violet-red tint.
Range Sri Lanka, Afghanistan, Brazil, Czech Republic, USA, Norway, India, Greenland, Tanzania, Madagascar.

MOHS'	SPEC GRAV	
7.5	4.2	

RHODOLITE

Although not the most common of the red garnets, rhodolite is the most valuable. It is formed in plutonic and ultra-mafic rocks, but due to its resistance to weathering, the crystals are usually found in alluvial secondary deposits or in arenaceous rocks. The crystal can vary in color and displays a strong luster and good transparency.

Mohs' Hardness 6.5–7.5.
Specific gravity 3.74–3.94.
Crystal structure Isometric.
Color Violet-blue, grayish-green.
Range Brazil, Sri Lanka, Tanzania, USA, Zambia, Zimbabwe.

MOHS'	SPEC GRAV	
7.5	3.94	

ZIRCON

An important source of zirconium, hafnium and thorium. Quality-grade crystals are cut into gemstones with green zircons being much in demand. Usually associated with acidic, igneous rocks or pegmatites. The crystals are four-sided and stubby, often perfectly transparent with good luster, but they can also be opaque and dull.

Mohs' Hardness 6.5–7.5.
Specific gravity 3.9–4.71.
Crystal structure Tetragonal.
Color Colorless to yellow.
Range Cambodia, Norway, Sri Lanka, Thailand, Vietnam, Australia, Brazil, USA.

MOHS'	SPEC GRAV
7.5	4.71

AXINITE

Named after the axle-like sharp edges which the stone usually displays when found. Quality crystals are sometimes cut into gemstones which have a modest value. Usually found within cavities in high-temperature granite or in contact metamorphic rocks. Crystals display a strong vitreous luster.

Mohs' Hardness 6.5–7.
Specific gravity 3.36–3.66.
Crystal structure Triclinic.
Color Deep-brownish-red, violet-red, brown, rose, yellow, red-orange, gray, green, blue.
Range France, Japan, Mexico, USA.

MOHS'	SPEC GRAV
7	3.66

AGATE

Agate is the name given to micro-crystalline quartz which is banded. These bands can be multicolored or different shades of the same color. Agates are nodules or geodes formed from gas-created voids which have become filled with silica in a volcanic environment. They usually have a white outer layer from weathering. If struck, they may chip or splinter.

Mohs' Hardness 6.5–7.
Specific gravity 2.60–2.65.
Crystal structure Hexagonal.
Color All colors, shades and hues.
Range Brazil, India, Uruguay, Canada, Germany, Russia, USA.

MOHS'
7

SPEC GRAV
2.65

JADE

Considered an Oriental stone, it has been used in America for thousands of years, as an ornamental material. Today it is still used for ornamental purposes but mainly with synthetic jade. Rarely found as a crystal, it is tough and translucent with a vitreous luster. Primarily found in veins, it also occurs as alluvial pebbles.

Mohs' Hardness 6.5–7.
Specific gravity 3.4.
Crystal structure Monoclinic.
Color Sea-green, off-white or grayish-white, brown, lilac, gray, orange-yellow.
Range Burma, China, Guatemala, Japan, Tibet, USA.

MOHS'
7

SPEC GRAV
3.4

CHALCEDONY

Chalcedony is the microcrystalline variety of quartz that forms concretional deposits. It is porous and can therefore be dyed. Natural crystals have no layering or banding.

Mohs' Hardness 6.5–7.
Specific gravity 2.58–2.64.
Crystal structure Hexagonal.
Color Blue whitish-gray, brownish-yellow, red, black, green, black-and-white, gray-and-white, yellow, red, brownish red or black.
Range Brazil, India, Madagascar, Uruguay.

MOHS'	SPEC GRAV	
7	2.64	

PERIDOT

Good quality, clear colored crystals are often cut and set with other gemstones. It is very widely distributed in iron- and magnesium-rich igneous rocks which form a continuous series. Crystals display a greasy vitreous luster when split, are usually transparent, and are not resistant to sulphuric acid.

Mohs' Hardness 6.5–7.
Specific gravity 3.27–4.20.
Crystal structure Orthorhombic.
Color Olive-green, bottle green, yellowish green or brown.
Range Zebirget in the Red Sea, USA, Hawaii, Australia, Brazil, South Africa.

MOHS'	SPEC GRAV	
7	4.20	

TANZANITE

Good quality crystals are sought after by jewelers and Tanzania's resources are almost exhausted. The crystals are formed as a result of the metamorphism of plagioclases. The coloration is due to the presence of chromium and strontium within the crystal structure. When heated, yellow and brown tints disappear and blue hues deepen.

Mohs' Hardness 6.5–7.
Specific gravity 3.11–3.40.
Crystal structure Orthorhombic.
Color Ultramarine to sapphire blue, violet, amethyst.
Range Tanzania.

MOHS'	SPEC GRAV
7	3.40

VESUVIANITE

Popular with jewelers, vesuvianite occurs as a product of contact metamorphism, or from mafic ejections. They are usually opaque, but translucent and transparent varieties usually have a vitreous to resinous luster. Crystals fuse easily and are virtually insoluble in acid.

Mohs' Hardness 6.5.
Specific gravity 3.27–3.45.
Crystal structure Tetragonal.
Color Brown to green, olive-green, yellow, blue, red or white.
Range Italy, Pakistan, USA, Norway, Russia.

MOHS'	SPEC GRAV
6.5	3.45

SINHALITE

Until 1952, sinhalite was thought to be brown-colored peridot, but it was noticed that the density was slightly higher, and X-ray crystallography showed it to be a different mineral. Sinhalite has distinct pleochroism, showing the colors, pale brown, greenish-brown and dark brown.

Mohs' Hardness 6.5.
Specific gravity 3.48.
Crystal structure Orthorhombic.
Color Pale yellow-brown to dark greenish-brown.
Range Sri Lanka, Burma, USA.

MOHS'	SPEC GRAV
6.5	3.48

ANDRADITE

Two varieties have been used in jewelry: opaque black melanite and green demantoid garnet. Melanite crystals are usually dodecahedra or icositetrahedra or a mixture of both. Demantoid is a very rare form of andradite, with a higher dispersion than a diamond, but the vivid green color masks this property. It is relatively soft and so is not commonly used in jewelry.

Mohs' Hardness 6.5.
Specific gravity 3.48.
Crystal structure Orthorhombic.
Color Pale yellow-brown to dark greenish-brown.
Range Sri Lanka, Burma, USA.

MOHS'	SPEC GRAV	
6.5	**3.48**	

EPIDOTE

Epidote is sometimes polished and used for inlay work; other crystals are occasionally used as gemstones. They are formed in metamorphic rocks of mafic composition. Piemontite and clinozoisite are the two varieties. It frequently occurs as a secondary hydrothermal alteration. The crystals are transparent with a vitreous lustre.

Mohs' Hardness 6–7.
Specific gravity 3.3–3.5.
Crystal structure Monoclinic.
Colour Full-green to yellow or brown-black, cherry-red, purplish-brown.
Range Austria, Norway, USA.

MOHS'
7

SPEC GRAV
3.5

AMAZONITE

Frequently confused with jade or turquoise, amazonite is often ground into beads for necklaces or made into ornamental objects. The crystals are normally squat and slightly prismatic and are found in metamorphic, intrusive and pegmatic rocks. It usually has a mottled appearance and can have a fine criss-cross network of light striations. They are generally opaque, with poor lustre.

Mohs' Hardness 6–6.5.
Specific gravity 2.56–2.58.
Crystal structure Triclinic.
Colour Light green, blue-green or bluish.
Range Australia, Brazil, India, Namibia, Madagascar, Russia, USA, Zimbabwe.

MOHS'
6.5

SPEC GRAV
2.58

BENITOITE

Benito crystals, sometimes confused with light colored sapphires, are often cut into gemstones. The crystals are found in veins in the brecciated body of a blue schist associated with serpentinite. The crystals, which are usually stubby and zoned, can look blue when viewed throught the acute faces of the rhombohedron, and colorless when viewed throught the obtuse faces.

Mohs' Hardness 6–6.5.
Specific gravity 3.65–3.68.
Crystal structure Hexagonal.
Color Light to dark blue.
Range San Benito county, California.

MOHS'
6.5

SPEC GRAV
3.68

SCAPOLITE

Scapolite is part of a continuous compositional series from calcium-rich to sodium-rich. The crystals are prismatic with three directions of easy cleavage. The luster varies from vitreous to resinous. The Burmese scapolite is cut *en cabochon* to show the cat's eye effect, while the Brazilian yellow scapolite is usually faceted.

Mohs' Hardness 6.
Specific gravity 2.60–2.70.
Crystal structure Tetragonal.
Color White, pink, violet, blue, yellow.
Range Burma, Brazil, Madagascar, Canada, Kenya.

MOHS'	SPEC GRAV	
6	2.70	

LABRADORITE

Usually fashioned into boxes or *objets d'art,* smaller specimens are made into beads, brooches or ring stones. It is associated with eruptive and metamorphic rocks. The most distinctive feature of labradorite is its iridescence against a dark background. This effect is probably caused by light on twinned lamellae.

Mohs' Hardness 6–6.5.
Specific gravity 2.62–2.76.
Crystal structure Triclinic.
Color Dark smoke-gray, but when light strikes it rainbow colors are displayed.
Range Canada, Madagascar, Mexico, Russia, USA.

MOHS'	SPEC GRAV	
6.5	2.76	

MOONSTONE

Moonstones display a blue reflection and can be confused with heat-treated amethysts or milky synthetic spinel. A variety of feldspar it is formed in association with orthoclase and albit. Almost colorless, it has only a pale-gray or yellow tint, with a whitish to silvery-white or blue shimmer.

Mohs' Hardness 6–6.5.
Specific gravity 2.56–2.62.
Crystal structure Monoclinic.
Color Colorless.
Range Australia, Burma, Sri Lanka, India, USA, Tanzania.

MOHS'
6.5

SPEC GRAV
2.62

OPAL

Opal is a hardened jelly made up of silica and water, found filling cavities in rocks, as stalagmites or as shell or bone. It has an uneven or conchoidal fracture. The iridescence is due to the interference of white light on minute silica spheres in the structure of the opal. Fire opals are usually faceted, while others are carved or cut *en cabochon*.

Mohs' Hardness 6.
Specific gravity 2.10.
Crystal structure Amorphous.
Color White, black, fire, water opal.
Range Europe, Guatemala, Honduras, Mexico, Australia, Brazil, South Africa.

MOHS'	SPEC GRAV
6	2.10

SPHENE

Gem-quality sphene is also known as titanite. The crystals are found as wedge shapes and are often twinned. They are brittle and have a weak cleavage. Sphene has very high 'fire' and the birefringence is high enough for doubling of the back facets to be seen with ease. It is usually cut as brilliant or mixed-cut gems to show its best effect.

Mohs' Hardness 5.5.
Specific gravity 3.52–3.54.
Crystal structure Monoclinic.
Color Yellow, brown, green.
Range Austria, Switzerland, Canada, Madagascar, Burma, California, Brazil.

MOHS'	SPEC GRAV	
5.5	**3.54**	

ORTHOCLASE

In its purest form, it is transparent and colorless and is a collector's gemstone. There are two directions of cleavage. Yellow orthoclase owes its color to the presence of iron, and is doubly refractive. It commonly occurs in intrusive, magmatic and metamorphic rocks where it has cooled slowly. Usually faceted as step-cut stones, it shows a cat's eye effect when cut en cabochon.

Mohs' Hardness 6.
Specific gravity 2.55–2.63.
Crystal structure Monoclinic.
Color Yellow, colorless, pinkish-brown.
Range Madagascar, Germany, USA.

MOHS'	SPEC GRAV	
6	2.63	

OLIGOCLASE

A member of the plagioclase felspar group. The variety shown here, sunstone, has reflective inclusions of red, orange or green thin platy crystals of hematite or goethite within an almost colorless oligoclase base. It has a vitreous luster.

Mohs' Hardness 6–6.5.
Specific gravity 2.64.
Crystal structure Triclinic.
Color Gray, white, greenish, yellowish, reddish, brown or colorless.
Range USA, Canada, Norway, India.

MOHS'	SPEC GRAV	
6.5	2.64	

HEMATITE

Hematite was used for mourning jewelry but is now used a a ring stone and in bead necklaces. A fairly common mineral, it is deposited in hydrothermal veins or in lavas. The crystals can be blood-red in thin sections. A heavy crystal, it is fragile and does not have any cleavage planes.

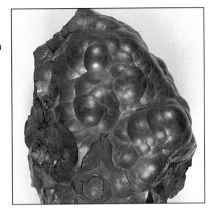

Mohs' Hardness 5.5–6.5.
Specific gravity 4.95–5.30.
Crystal structure Hexagonal.
Color Black, dark iron-gray.
Range Angola, Brazil, Canada, USA.

MOHS'	SPEC GRAV	
6.5	**5.30**	

SODALITE

Often confused with lapis lazuli, it occurs in under-saturated plutonic rocks, asscociated with metamorphosed limestones and volcanic rocks. The crystals are fragile with poor cleavage and translucent with vitreous luster. The presence of sodium is shown by a yellow flame when the crystals fuse.

Mohs' Hardness 5.5–6.
Specific gravity 2.13–2.33.
Crystal structure Isometric.
Color Bright blue to violet, from white to gray with green tints.
Range Brazil, Canada, Bolivia, Burma, Greenland, India, Romania, Portugal.

MOHS'	SPEC GRAV	
6	**2.33**	

LAZULITE

Also known as lapis lazuli, it has been used as an ornamental stone for thousands of years in *objets d'art*. It is an uncommon mineral, occurring with metamorphosed limestone. It polishes well but is fragile and breaks imperfectly. Porous, it may be treated with paraffin to enhance the blue color.

Mohs' Hardness 5–6.
Specific gravity 2.38–2.9.
Crystal structure Isometric.
Color Blue.
Range Afghanistan, Chile, Russia, Angola, Burma, Canada, Pakistan, USA.

MOHS'
6

SPEC GRAV
2.9

TURQUOISE

Primarily used for making necklaces, brooches, amulets and *objets d'art*. It is a secondary mineralization and is rich in apatite and chalcopyrite. Turquoises usually occur as grape- or kidney-shaped aggregates, and are soluble in hydrochloric acid.

Mohs' Hardness 5–6.
Specific gravity 2.6–2.9.
Crystal structure Triclinic.
Color Blue-white to sky-blue, light greenish-blue to light blue.
Range Iran, USA.

MOHS'
6

SPEC GRAV
2.9

BRAZILIANITE

A rare and beautiful crystal which is much prized by jewelers and collectors. They occur in cavities in pegmatites associated with blue apatite, clay and lazulite. The crystals are usually elongated and stubby prisms and can be quite large. They are fragile with perfect cleavage, and are transparent with a vitreous luster.

Mohs' Hardness 5.5.
Specific gravity 2.98–2.99.
Crystal structure Monoclinic.
Color Yellow or green-yellow.
Range Brazil, USA.

MOHS'	SPEC GRAV	
5.5	**2.99**	

DIOPSIDE

Transparent specimens of diopside can be cut into gems. The crystals are formed from contact metamorphism associated with other calcium silicates. Varieties are violane, purple, chromian diopside, dark-green and lavrovite. The crystals are fragile with perfect prismatic cleavage and translucent with a vitreous luster.

Mohs' Hardness 5–6.
Specific gravity 3.27–3.31.
Crystal structure Monoclinic.
Color White, yellow, green, blue, brown, colorless.
Range Austria, Finland, Greenland, South Africa, Madagascar, Sweden.

MOHS'	SPEC GRAV	
6	**3.31**	

DIOPTASE

Dioptase is used for making jewelry and is popular with crystal collectors. It occurs as short prismatic crystals within cavities in the oxidation zones of copper deposits. The crystals are fragile with perfect cleavage, and transparent with a vitreous luster.

Mohs' Hardness 5.
Specific gravity 3.28–3.35.
Crystal structure Hexagonal.
Color Bright emerald-green.
Range Chile, Namibia, Russia, Zaire, USA.

MOHS'	SPEC GRAV	
5	3.35	

HEMIMORPHITE

Primarily a zinc ore, hemimorphite can be cut and set as gemstones or used for decorative fabrication. It is formed in the oxidized zones of lead and zinc deposits. Rarely found as large crystals, more commonly found as platex crystals whose ends are different or hemimorphic.

Mohs' Hardness 4.5–5.
Specific gravity 3.4–3.5.
Crystal structure Orthorhombic.
Color White, transparent or translucent, with tints of yellow, green, blue or brownish-blue.
Range Algeria, Greece, Italy, Namibia, Mexico, USA.

MOHS'	SPEC GRAV	
5	3.5	